LEARNING
ABOUT
Union With Christ

Stewart Dinnen

Christian Focus

ISBN 1 85792 424 X

© Stewart Dinnen

Published in 2000
by
Christian Focus Publications
Geanies House, Fearn,
Ross-shire, IV20 1TW, Great Britain

Cover Design by Owen Daily

Contents

SOME BOOKS THAT EXPLAIN
UNION WITH CHRIST

Anderson N.T. *The Bondage Breaker*, Harvest House, Eugene, OR, 1990, or Monarch, Speldhurst, Kent, 1993

——*The Steps to Freedom in Christ*, Gospel Light, Glendale, 1996

——*Victory Over the Darkness*, Gospel Light, Ventura, 1990, or Monarch, Speldhurst, Kent, 1992

Benson R. & M. *Disciplines of the Inner Life*, Word, Waco, TX, 1985

Dinnen S. (Ed.), *Summit Living,* CLC, Fort Washington, 1985 (Daily Readings from the writings of Norman Grubb)

Gordon A.J., *In Christ*, Moody, Chicago, 1972

Grubb N.P., *God Unlimited*, Lutterworth, London, 1962

——*Once Caught, No Escape*, Lutterworth, London, 1969

——*The Spontaneous You*, Lutterworth, London, 1966

——*Yes, I Am*, CLC, Fort Washington, 1986

Hegre T., *The Three Aspects of the Cross*, Bethany Press, Minneapolis

Huegel F.J., *Bone of His Bone*, Zondervan, Grand Rapids, 1972

Reigning With Christ, Zondervan, Grand Rapids, 1962

Lawrence Bro., *The Practice of the Presence Of God*, Whitaker House, Springdale, PA, 1982

Murray A., *Abide in Christ*, Oliphants, London, 1968

Nee W., *The Normal Christian Life*, Gospel Literature Service, Bombay, 1957

——*The Release of the Spirit*, Gospel Literature Service, Bombay, 1964

Penn-Lewis J., *The Message of the Cross*, Overcomer Trust, Dorset

——*The Centrality of the Cross*, Overcomer Trust, Dorset

INTRODUCTION

The wonderful theme of *Union with Christ* has been close to my heart for many years. It first dawned on me through the ministry and writings of Norman Grubb, the man whom God used to develop WEC International after its foundation by C. T. Studd. Out of concern for us as new workers in the mission, and probably sensing our spiritual need, he sent my wife and me to Swansea, Wales, to sit under the teaching of Rees Howells, a mighty man of intercession. As a result he also had a profound influence upon our lives.

The third person whom God used to lever us into a deeper walk with God was Ted Hegre, founder and leader of the Bethany Fellowship in Minneapolis, whose book *The Message of the Cross* is now a spiritual classic.

Those familiar with these three men will soon spot emphases that can be traced back to them, and I give an unashamed acknowledgement of this.

In helping to train young people for Christian service I made extensive use of the insights thus gained, but of course, they had to be hammered out on the anvil of practical Christian living before the watching eyes of fifty, sixty or seventy students and fellow staff members in a residential college setting.

I am totally convinced that these teachings saved us from a very humdrum, run-of-the-mill Christian experience, and liberated us into a lifestyle that has been adventurous, exciting and totally satisfying, over the years since first they dawned upon us.

Stewart Dinnen,
Launceston, Tasmania,
July, 1999

CHAPTER 1

THIS WAY TO FREEDOM

'Peter' was leader of a large overseas field in a mission majoring in evangelism and church planting. High in the Himalayas, the annual staff conference had come around and once again he was flat out attending to organisational details.

But a visitor from another mission who had been invited to give the devotional talks detected the stress in his demeanour.

At a quiet moment he pulled him aside. 'Peter, I think you're carrying your job with human energy, not out of a restful reliance on the Lord. Take a look at Galatians 2:20.'

Alone in his room later, he cried to the Lord, and prostrating his body on the floor so that it took the shape of a cross, he accepted the truth of being crucified and risen with Christ. His leadership was transformed and he went on to become the international director of his mission with responsibility for hundreds of workers around the world.

Norman Grubb describes how, as young and new missionaries, he and his wife sat up late one night in the Congo moonlight trying to understand teaching about the Cross in a booklet by Mrs Penn-Lewis, sent to him from England. Dissatisfied with their current level of effectiveness, both entered by faith into an acceptance of the Cross principle and of the resurrection life available in the Lord. Next morning he took a blank card, drew a tombstone and inscribed the words 'Here lieth Norman Grubb, buried with Jesus'. They went on to become – against incredible odds – God's instruments in the amazing development of WEC International.

David (not his real name) had joined a well known mission agency and was full of enthusiasm for the tasks that came his way. But he ran into trouble: his 'pushiness' put people off. In staff meetings his forcefulness in bulldozing his ideas through, alienated and offended others who held different viewpoints.

A glimmer of light started to penetrate when a senior worker pulled him aside. 'David, you come through so dogmatically that you put others off. You are losing friends, fast!'

Transferred to another department (and somewhat chastened), he vowed to take a lower profile in discussions. Because of his communication gifts he was often 'up front' in public meetings, but here also he ran into trouble. His manner was counter-productive.

Once again there was a thoughtful senior worker who was genuinely concerned for him.

'David, first the good news. You are a talented fellow and we are glad you are part of the team, but the bad news is that you come over as operating out of human strength rather than in humble dependence on the Holy Spirit. Too much David. Not enough Jesus! I don't think you have seen the Cross principle yet.'

This time the message really penetrated. He retreated to his room where the Spirit gave him a revelation of his self-reliance and unbrokenness. He acknowledged his self-sufficiency and told the Lord he really did want to operate only in the power of the Spirit.

That was the turning point. He started to know a new freedom and an enabling that led eventually to him being given great responsibilities in Christian service.

The pattern of these experiences is easily seen: an awareness of inadequacy that leads to an acceptance of the Cross as a principle and a basic deliverance from self-reliance; an entering in by faith into the total sufficiency of Christ's resurrection life; then a new era of effectiveness and victory in the work of God's Kingdom.

When we look at the experience of the Israelites in the Old Testament – and 1 Corinthians 10:13 justifies us in taking these events as typifying the New Testament believer's spiritual pilgrimage – we find the same three phases.

Moses, as he reviews the nation's past

experience and then looks into the future says (Deut. 6:23-7:2): 'He brought us out from there (Egypt) that He might bring us in, to give us the land (Canaan). When the Lord brings you into the land... you shall conquer them (many nations) and utterly destroy them.' Here are the three stages: Freedom, Fulness and Effectiveness.

They correlate exactly with the New Testament's teaching on the believer's union with Christ in his death, resurrection and ascension.

Look at Colossians 3:3: 'You died, and your life is hidden with Christ in God' (union in Christ's death); Colossians 3:1: 'If then you were raised with Christ' (union with Christ's resurrection life); Colossians 3:1: 'Seek those things which are above, where Christ is sitting at the right hand of God' (union in His ascended position). If you think this is a far-fetched interpretation, just look at Paul's description of the Christian worker in 2 Corinthians 4 where he states and repeats his position regarding his union with Christ in death and resurrection. Verse 10: 'Always carrying about in the body the dying of the Lord Jesus that the life of Jesus also may be manifested in our body.' Verse 11: 'We who live are always delivered to death for Jesus' sake, that the life of Jesus also may be manifested in our mortal flesh.' Verse 12: 'Death is at work in us, but life in you.' The last verse of the chapter expresses his viewpoint from the ascended position, 'We do not look at things which are seen but at the things which are not seen.... The things that are not seen are eternal.'

When Paul reveals his innermost longings, what subject is uppermost? His union with Christ. '...that I may know him and the power of his resurrection and the fellowship of his sufferings being conformed to his death' (Phil. 3:10), and then in verse 20 he asserts his union with Christ at the throne, 'For our citizenship is in heaven.'

Nowhere is the resurrection union and the ascended position stated more clearly than in Ephesians 2:6: '...raised us up together and made us sit together in the heavenly places', and in chapter 6:12 Paul describes our position in the spiritual battle against satanic forces: 'we do not wrestle against flesh and blood but against principalities and powers...'

Specific passages in which union in His death is expounded come in Romans where Paul shows that we are dead to sin (chapter 6), the law (chapter 7), and to independent self (chapter 8).

His Galatian letter is very explicit and states his testimony once again. 'I have been crucified with Christ. It is no longer I who lives but Christ lives in me, and the life which I now live in the flesh I live by faith in the Son of God, who loved me and gave himself for me' (2:20).

Is this union concept confined to Paul? No. Peter mentions the same theme when he says in 1

Peter 2:24,25: 'Who himself bore our sins in his body on the tree that we, *having died to sin* (i.e. in union with Christ) *might live for righteousness* (i.e. in Christ's resurrection life).

In John 12:24 and 25 Jesus taught union with Himself, firstly in His death where He describes Himself as a grain of wheat falling into the ground and dying, and immediately applies the same truth to His disciples in the next verse. Verse 25 also mentions sharing eternal (resurrection) life with Him, and verse 26 indicates life in the heavenlies with Him – 'Where I am, there my servant will be also.'

CHAPTER 2

A PILE-UP OF IMAGES

How does identification with Christ bring freedom and deliverance? The fact is that when we accept the cross as a principle (there was only one cross *event*) we are committing ourselves to a *dying out* to the power of sin.

This is the whole point of Paul's detailed teaching in Romans 6. When the word 'die' is used in its verbal form it is *apothnesko* in the Greek. The root, *thnesko*, means 'to die' and the prefix, *apo,* means 'from'. So, the essential idea here is not obliteration but simply a 'dying out' to sin – a position made real in our experience by faith. The imagery of the passage confirms this. Baptism (verse 4), literally means being totally immersed in His death. 'Buried' is *sunthapto; sun*, the prefix, meaning 'together with', and *thapto*, 'to bury'. 'United' (verse 5) is *sumphuo; sum,* 'together with', and *phuo,* 'implant'. (It was a term used in gardening when a scion was grafted into a branch of the mother tree.) 'Was crucified' uses the verb *sustauroo; sus* meaning 'together with' and *stauroo* meaning 'to crucify'.

What does this build-up of imagery convey? Paul was, in effect, saying, 'Because by faith you are a new creature in Christ, God sees you as having dropped out of the old bondage to sin.' This puts us in the incredible position of being able to resist evil, not because we are clever or have a strong will, but because we can affirm the broken relationship to sin and the new union with Christ's resurrection life. We overcome by faith in the facts! We are 'drop-outs' as far as the power of sin is concerned!

In verses 1-11 Paul appeals to our spiritual understanding by using words like 'know' (verses 3, 6, 9), 'believe' (verse 8), 'reckon' (verse 11). In verses 12-23 he appeals to our will, the key words here being 'present' (verses 13, 16, 19), 'obey' (verses 16, 17), 'be a slave to' (verses 16, 18, 19, 20, 22). In effect he is saying, first, 'understand your new position', then 'assert the truth of it, in experience'. Holiness therefore is not a kind of achievement, but a 'cashing in' on the power and dynamic of the new relationship.

Norman Grubb, in his book, *Yes I am* (page 72), writes:

But to consider myself *dead to sin* is no light thing, especially when I do not yet appear to experience it. We hesitate to declare 'I am dead to sin', because we are thinking about how often sin still seems to turn up in us. But the issue is plain. Will we obey God's Word? In this same chapter, Paul says that we have 'obeyed from the heart that form of doctrine which was delivered unto us'. Have we, really? So let us 'go to it' and be sure we boldly affirm and declare what His Word says we are. Let us not compromise (as many folks do – even teachers of the Bible) and seek to get around this by saying it is our 'position' but not yet our 'condition' – a lovely little evangelical wriggle. Let us rather obey, and declare what we are told to *recognise, attend to,* and *say.* Then let us go further, after our word of faith and obedience, and find out how this *is* a present fact in condition as well as position.

With our whole self totally and solely at His disposal we joyfully recognise our new Owner. Because of His new management within us, the old owner, Satan, has no control over us. He can shout at us from without, but he has no further place within. We have changed bosses! We are in the employment of a new Firm!

The Scottish theologian, James Denney, in his book *The Death of Christ* (page 106) comes at this truth from a different angle, yet reaches, broadly, the same conclusion. He writes:

The very same experience in which a man becomes right with God, that is, the experience of faith in Christ who died for sins, is an experience in which he becomes a dead man so far as sin is concerned and a living man (though this is but the same thing in other words) so far as God is concerned. As long as faith is at its normal tension the life of sin is inconceivable.

An interesting passage confirming this 'death to sin' and at the same time containing the requirement that we take action in line with it is found in Colossians 3. The *fact* of our death with Christ is stated in verse 9, '...you *have put off* the old man', yet the appeal to the will to ratify such a position is given in verse 8, '*put off*... anger, wrath, malice...'

The same double thrust is made on the positive side: '...(you) *have put on* the new man...' (verse 10), and then comes the injunction in verse 12: '*put on* tender mercies, kindness, humility...'

We are in a position to 'produce the goods' morally, only when we have first committed ourselves by faith to the fact of our union in Christ's death and resurrection.

'Jim' attended a youth camp where the speaker was laying out the truths of our identification with Christ in His death and resurrection. He struggled over the teaching as it was not taught in the church where he was a member.

At the end of the weekend he approached the speaker. 'I don't think I've really grasped what you have been saying. It's all pretty new to me.' The man who had given the messages said, 'It's good that you are concerned, Jim. Here are a few more Scriptures that may help.... And I'll be praying for you.'

Some weeks later a letter from Jim reached the camp speaker. Part of it said: 'I've seen what you were trying to get over, and I have really entered by faith into this inner union. I also realise that my decision to go into accountancy some years ago was my own idea, and not the Lord's, so I am praying over my whole future.' (He had just finished his course at that time).

Some months later he moved into a Bible College, then into a seminary, and eventually he served the Lord in Africa where he commenced a Bible School for nationals.

The diagram on the next page is an attempt to clarify the meaning and purpose of the Cross as a propitiation (sacrifice for sin), a principle, and as a pattern. We are saved through believing in Christ who died for our sin. We *should* then move on to accepting the principle of the Cross as taught by Jesus in Luke 14:27, but many miss out on this (as Jim did) and remain what is described in 1 Corinthians 3:1 as carnal, fleshly or worldly. They are described in the same verse as spiritual 'babes' – they have never grown. But when the Cross principle is accepted then the Spirit-disciplined life commences and in His strength we become effective and stay useful because we are willing for the daily dying to self – the Cross pattern.

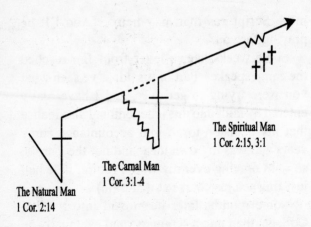

The Spiritual Man
1 Cor. 2:15, 3:1

The Carnal Man
1 Cor. 3:1-4

The Natural Man
1 Cor. 2:14

THE CROSS	THE CROSS	THE CROSS
- A PROPITIATION	- A PRINCIPLE	- A PATTERN
(sacrifice for sin)	(the termination of an independent lifestyle)	(a daily dying to self)
"The Son of God loved me and gave himself for me."	"I have been crucified with Christ. Nevertheless I live; yet not I but Christ lives in me."	"Being confromed to his death."
Gal. 2:20b	Gal. 2:20a	Phil. 3:10

The diagram is simplified in order to delineate the different concepts of the Cross, but of course, long-term experience is not necessarily in that strictly chronological sequence. As we grow in the Lord we will keep returning and entering into a deeper understanding of all three meanings.

CHAPTER 3

THE INNER KNOWING

Just as Romans 6 explains deliverance from sin, chapter 7 explains deliverance from law. In many ways this is a more subtle threat to the 'works'-oriented believer, who knows that he is forgiven and cleansed, and feels that it is now up to him to show his appreciation for salvation by trying to keep to a certain standard. Laudable – but impossible, because that kind of thinking is based on the concept of separation, not union. Under law, I try to do something for God. Under grace, I allow Christ to live His life through me. Under law, I am on the treadmill of effort; under grace I am borne along by the Spirit. The will is still active, but it is active in maintaining a relationship, not earning a reward.

Law is any external pressure on us to conform to a standard. Law can only appeal to the flesh (self-effort) not to Christ in me because Christ is the end of the law for righteousness to everyone who believes (Romans 10:4). In verse 6 Paul says, 'We have been delivered from the law having died to what we were held by, so that we should serve in the newness of the Spirit and not in the oldness of the letter.'

Paul confirms this when he says in Galatians 2:19, 20: 'For I through the law died to the law that I might live to God. I have been crucified with Christ; it is no longer I who lives but Christ lives in me.'

The *standards* of the law have, of course, never been rescinded, but *obligation* to the law and motivation by the law ended when we trusted in Christ.

'Steve' used to be in bondage to the obligation to witness. Of course we should witness, but when it is done out of a sense of duty the blessing is not in it because God can't bless the effort of the flesh. Once this was understood, he relaxed in situations of potential witnessing and then openings started to come. Sitting next to a businessman on a plane he wondered how God would create an opening. It came, as the following conversation reveals:

'Have you ever heard of Billy Graham?' said the stranger.

'Yes, I have.'

'Well, my wife is a Billy Graham fanatic and I am just bewildered by it all.'

'Well, as a matter of fact I am, too. I'm a born again believer.'

'Oh no...'

'Oh yes. Probably your wife is praying that you'll get a seat on the plane next to a Christian, and here I am!'

And so the conversation continued – all the way to their destination!

Romans 8 deals with deliverance from 'the flesh'. What is it? It is self-reliant, independent action. Christians can and do act independently of the grace of God. Very often our negative reactions to wrong treatment by others come right out of a sense of self-vindication. What is this? Purely an expression of independent self. Paul called people who behaved like this 'carnal'. He also called them 'brothers' – so they were Christians, but were being activated by self. (1 Cor. 3:1)

The whole point of Romans 8 is to show that holiness (the righteous requirements of the law) is possible through walking *in the Spirit*. 'For if you live according to the flesh you will die; but if by the Spirit you put to death the deeds of the body, you will live' (verse 13).

So there is for us a dying – a putting to death of the deeds (activity) of the body (which can be the vehicle of independent action) and there is an entering into the life of the Spirit. There is a by-faith plunge into this realm of reality. For many it is just a wetting of the toes – an occasional experience of it – but if we persist we start to feel 'waters to swim in', and living with this inner restfulness becomes a sub-conscious reality.

If the truth be known, probably a good percentage of our praying is taken up with asking the Lord to be what He has already promised to be!

Do we sense, then, that the issue is settled? That we are living with an *inner knowing* that He is indeed our life, and our lifegiver? That we are delivered from the strivings of self-reliant self?

Here is Norman Grubb's testimony as he moved from seeing this truth to the point where it became an inner reality:

I did not lightly move into my part of the believing. After five night-hours of battling around with it (so little did I understand the ease of faith in those days), I did finally put my finger on Galatians 2:20, or at least on the first phrase of it, and said right out, 'I am crucified with Christ.'

But did I feel different or know anything different? No. My precious wife, Pauline, was with me and did the same. We had those five hours sitting in our little camp chairs in the forest, in the banana plantation of a precious African brother we had gone to visit. But the Spirit responded more quickly to Pauline. Within two weeks she felt what she took to be a touch on her shoulder, beneath the mosquito net on her camp bed. It was the Spirit confirming her word of faith, and she knew and has known ever since. Next morning, as we sat outside the little native hut we had been staying in, breakfasting at our camp table, she began to say to me that she had something to tell me; but I said, 'No need, your face shows it' – and her life has shown it all these years since.

But for me, perhaps because I was more a 'thinker-through' of a thing, and a slower believer, it wasn't until two years later that the inner light was turned on in my consciousness. During those two years I never went back on that crisis of affirming faith. It had been as serious to me as a wedding ceremony (yes, faith is a serious business). So it was background fact to me as I continued my missionary village travellings. But not until I was home on furlough, and speaking with Mrs. Penn-Lewis, a woman of God whose writings had first helped me into this understanding of Romans 6–8 and Galatians 2:20, was this light inwardly turned on in me.

The point to me was not her story but that as she spoke, *I knew*: How? I didn't know. But I *knew*, and that was a great number of years ago. And *I still know*. Just as certainly and clearly as I knew by the inner witness on the day I came to Christ that I was born again. That's how I know; and you know, or will know in God's time. He confirms what we have affirmed. That's all.

But I do know that as He thus became inwardly real to me, as the One living my life, I did move into an inner knowing which was and is equivalent to saying, *It is He living in me and not I.*

(From *Yes, I am*, chapter 21, pp 101-102, published by Christian Literature Crusade.)

CHAPTER 4

STILL FURTHER FREEDOM

Union goes even further. Not only are we one with Christ in His death as a dying out to sin, law and the flesh; we have another area of deliverance shown to us by Paul, when he says in Galatians 6:14: 'God forbid that I should boast except in the cross of our Lord Jesus Christ, by whom the world has been crucified to me, and I to the world.'

But what is 'the world'? Yes, it is the place where we live, but Paul wasn't meaning that. He was meaning the *world system*, and Scripture in 1 John 2:16 gives us an excellent definition of this system – the lust of the flesh (inordinate greed for gain and for sex), the lust of the eyes (greed for what we can see – material things), and the pride of life (greed for position, power and influence). Gain is not wrong, sex is not wrong, material comforts are not wrong – but when our lifestyle is motivated and dominated by greed for these then we are living in the world.

A young, newly qualified accountant sat in a missionary convention as the writer brought biblical teaching on the meaning of discipleship. Afterwards he said: 'I've just obtained a wonderful position and have great prospects but when you talked about being double-minded the word flew into my heart. I need to go home and sort this out. Pray for me.'

The world system was beckoning him. Now having a good job isn't wrong but if its strong allurement keeps us from surrendering to the lordship of Christ then it becomes wrong.

A young airline mechanic in a church one day listened to a speaker challenging the Christians about knowing the will of God. He used an illustration from the Canadian timber industry, where huge trees are felled, branches lopped off and the logs are taken to a river where they are floated downstream to the mill. Occasionally a log escapes the system and floats out to the estuary where it becomes a danger to small craft. Then the speaker said, 'Are you a "drifting log" as far as God's purposes are concerned?' The Holy Spirit convicted this young man because that was exactly what he was. He was being driven along within the world system. He started to pray earnestly for an understanding of the Lord's will for him and felt led to apply for Bible training. When he submitted his resignation to the airline they called him in. 'Why take this foolish step? You have your engineer's certificate. You have your private pilot's licence. You are working towards your commercial licence and once you have that the company will train you to pilot the big jets. Don't give all that away.'

But God's call was clear. What the company was suggesting to him constituted a worldly allurement to which he had to apply the Cross principle. He became a missionary and today is principal of a college, training others to serve the Lord.

There is one more aspect of deliverance that we obtain through union with Christ. That is Christ's dying (and rising) to break the power of Satan in human life.

If you are asked 'Why did Jesus die?', what is your answer? 'He died for the sins of the world.' 'His death was to redeem us from the penalty of sin.' 'His death was a means of appeasing God's anger.' All these are correct but not the full answer. Scripture teaches that Jesus in His dying and rising from the dead was breaking Satan's power, that is, making victory over his assaults possible for the believer.

Hebrews 2:14 and 15 is a profound passage. John Owen, the Puritan theologian, describes its message as 'The death of death in the death of Christ'. We can paraphrase it as follows: 'Christ came and shared our humanity so that in dying He might render powerless the one who had the power of death – Satan – and so be able to release those who are in bondage to the fear of dying.'

Another verse that confirms this is 1 John 3:8, a paraphrase of the second half being: 'The reason that the Son of God came and revealed Himself was in order to loose us from Satan's activities.'

A succinct sentence in Revelation 12:11 summarises this truth very neatly: 'They overcame him (Satan) by the blood of the Lamb.' In other words what Jesus did at the Cross makes victory over Satan possible – not, please note, automatic, but possible by faith in the efficacy of His sacrifice. It is this fact that makes James 4:7 a reality - 'Resist the Devil and he will flee...' (See chapter 7 for a further development of this, and for an explanation of our authority in Christ.)

Peter Wagner relates how in 1985 a group of pastors in Argentina made a survey of an area within a 100 mile radius of their city, Rosario, and found 104 towns without an evangelical church. They also discovered a group of satanists in one town who seemed to be dominating this area with their evil practices. The pastors went to the town where this group had its base and had a powerful time of prayer, binding Satan and claiming victory, on the basis of 1 John 3:8. Today every one of these towns has an evangelical church! (*Territorial Spirits, Sovereign World*, Chichester, 1991, page 49).

Colossians 2:15 says: 'Jesus disarmed principalities and powers. He made a public exhibition of them, being victorious over them in the Cross.'

'Irene', a Christian worker in Africa, describes how she has had victory over Satanic pressures through her union with Christ.

'The more I have weeded Satan's influence out of my heart, the more I have discovered who I really am. The biblical statements about me have become excitingly real. I am a new creature. I died with Christ and am living in union with Him. I have a spirit of love, not fear.

'Some time ago I realised that the Spirit of God was not the only spirit expressing itself through me. I was horrified and ashamed. I asked God to confirm this to me, and three times in one day I heard myself uttering unkind words that were not my own and were most certainly not from the Spirit of God. Distressed, I talked to God about it. He showed me that Satan had gained a foothold through my intolerance. I asked God to forgive me. In the Name of Jesus I told Satan to take his intolerance out of my life. I found relief. I discovered that situations which would have previously made me angry or impatient no longer did so. It was good to be alerted to the fact that Satan could be illegally squatting in territory that rightly belongs to God.

'I also found to my astonishment that I was bound by fear. I had not considered myself to be fearful, but the Lord made me aware that dread would fill my heart from time to time, especially after I had performed some service for Him; I was afraid of failure. I felt pain in my stomach when I had prayed an audacious prayer; I was afraid of what people would think. He drew my attention to the way I would avoid people who had the gift of discernment; I was afraid of exposure. He showed me all these fears were of Satan. What a relief! How marvellous to know that I could be free of them and enjoy the peace that Jesus died to give me.

'Knowing who I am in Christ has revolutionised my life. I meet its challenges with confidence, knowing that Jesus lives His life in me.'

CHAPTER 5

TOTAL ADEQUACY

Up to this point we have been dealing with escape, rescue, freedom from everything that would hinder God's purposes in our lives. Now we are ready for stage two – the faith plunge into the total sufficiency of Christ's resurrection life made real to us by the Spirit. This is what Paul was concentrating on when he said in Philippians 3:10, 'That I may know him, and the power of his resurrection.'

Satan will do all he can to prevent us from entering into this rest-of-faith. His thrust right from the garden of Eden has been *separation*; Jesus' purpose is *union*. Satan's substitute for union is *self-effort*, and he may not mind when we use prayers like, 'Lord, be with me,' 'Lord, give me more grace,' 'Lord, help me to love that difficult person,' 'Lord, give me more love.' All of these can be prayers of unbelief, because the Scriptures assure us that we *have* all these by virtue of our union with Jesus. 'The love of God *has been* shed abroad in our hearts.' 'I am with you to the end of the age.' 'Jesus Christ [is] made unto us wisdom, righteousness, sanctification, redemption.' Why waste time asking Jesus to be what He has already promised to be in us?

Ephesians is the biblical book that more than any other reveals the hidden treasure of Christ's indwelling resurrection life. 'Blessed be the God and Father of our Lord Jesus Christ, who has blessed us with every spiritual blessing in the heavenlies in Christ' (1:3). 'The exceeding greatness of His power toward us who believe' (1:19). 'The unsearchable riches of Christ' (3:8).

Look at Paul's two prayers in chapters one and three. In 1:17-20 he is virtually saying, 'Lord, help them to realise all that they have in You.' He is not praying that they will *do* anything. He only asks that their faith-eyes will be opened to see what they already have! In 3:16-19 he develops the same idea, when he prays that, with Christ dwelling in their hearts by faith, they may, through Him, be 'filled with all the fullness of God'.

When we grasp this, the dominant characteristic of our lifestyle will be the *restfulness of faith*. The restful believer may be an intensely busy person, but there will be a consciousness of His sufficiency within. Battle – yes. Awareness of conflict – yes. Challenges to faith – of course. But they will all be accompanied by confidence in His total adequacy within.

This is when we come to a realisation of our supreme destiny – to be containers or channels or expressers of His divine life! This is the point of

Jesus's emphasis in John 15 – the branch totally dependent upon and lodged in the main stem, resulting in fruitfulness.

Let's imagine we can talk to that branch.

'Mr Branch, congratulations. That's a magnificent bunch of grapes you've produced this year.'

'Yes, pretty good, but don't congratulate me.'

'Why not? You've produced it! Can I taste one of your grapes?'

'Help yourself.'

'Hey, Branch, that's luscious! You must be an expert dietitian! And, by the way, I love the shape of the bunch. Symmetrical, cone-shaped. You're quite a designer!'

'Oh, I didn't think that up.'

'And look at the colours! That deep purple! The work of an artist!'

'Look, I'm no artist, designer or dietitian. I did one thing only.'

'What's that?'

'*I stayed in the main stem!* That's all. It's the lifesap flowing through the main stem and through me that has produced the fruit. I'm only a bit of plumbing for the lifesap. I just keep a good connection.'

Is the lifesap flowing? How's the connection? Is the union a reality, being kept vital and fresh by prayer and an ever-increasing grasp of His Word?

Note, from John 6, how deeply concerned Jesus is about having an intimate relationship with us. See how often He describes Himself as 'bread' or 'flesh' and 'blood'.

verse 32: 'My Father gives you the true bread from heaven.'

verse 33: 'The bread of God is he who comes down from heaven and gives life...'

verse 35: 'I am the bread of life.'

verse 48: 'I am the bread of life.'

verse 50: 'This is the bread which comes down from heaven.'

verse 51: 'I am the living bread. If anyone eats of this bread he will live forever.'

verse 53: 'Unless you eat of the flesh of the Son of Man and drink his blood you have no life in you.'

verse 54: 'Whoever eats my flesh and drinks my blood has eternal life.'

verse 55: 'My flesh is food indeed, and my blood is drink indeed.'

verse 56: 'He who eats my flesh and drinks my blood abides in me and I in him.'

verse 58: 'This is the bread which came down from heaven.'

Why did Jesus use such imagery and repeat it so often? Because He had found the perfect illustration of union. What happens to bread, or meat, or drink? They are assimilated into the body. Jesus qualifies this terminology when He says, a few verses later, 'The words that I speak to you are spirit, and they are life.' In other words He is saying that the previous verses are physical images of the inner spiritual union He wants to have with those who believe in Him.

The flow of His resurrection life results in the emergence of the fruit of the Spirit and the expression of a gift or gifts of the Spirit. (1 Corinthians 12:7 and 1 Peter 4:10 say we all have at least one gift.)

The fruit is the answer to the need for holiness and operates in three relationships – within myself, towards others, and towards God.

Gifts are given for the benefit of the local fellowship (1 Cor. 12:7), and are the Spirit's equipping for effective service. Not to use our gift or gifts is to rob the fellowship of our unique and distinctive contribution (1 Cor. 12:12-27).

CHRIST'S RESURRECTION LIFE

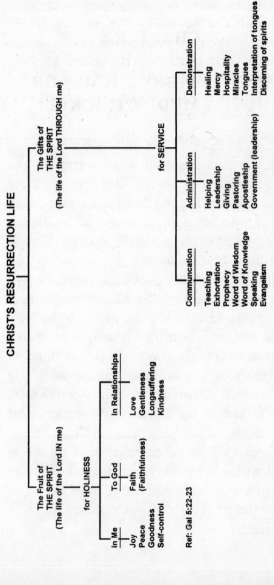

The Fruit of THE SPIRIT
(The life of the Lord IN me)

for HOLINESS

In Me
Joy
Peace
Goodness
Self-control

To God
Faith (Faithfulness)

In Relationships
Love
Gentleness
Longsuffering
Kindness

Ref: Gal 5:22-23

The Gifts of THE SPIRIT
(The life of the Lord THROUGH me)

for SERVICE

Communcation
Teaching
Exhortation
Prophecy
Word of Wisdom
Word of Knowledge
Speaking
Evangelism

Administration
Helping
Leadership
Giving
Pastoring
Apostleship
Government (leadership)

Demonstration
Healing
Mercy
Hospitality
Miracles
Tongues
Interpretation of tongues
Discerning of spirits

Ref: Rom. 12:6-8; 1 Cor. 12:7-12, 28; Eph. 4:11; 1 Pet. 4:10-11

CHAPTER 6

RIVERS THROUGH ME? OR JUST A MUDDY TRICKLE?

Wonderful though those truths about our union with Christ in His death and resurrection are, God's purpose is not fulfilled through these alone. We need to grasp the significance of being united with Jesus in His ascended position if we are to move on into God's strategy. We can call this 'life at the throne'.

It is a thoroughly Biblical concept. Paul in Colossians 3:1-3 says, 'Seek those things which are above, where Christ is, sitting at the right hand of God.' Then he virtually repeats this injunction in the next verse. 'Set your mind on things above, not on things on the earth.' He deals with it also in Ephesians 2:6 when he says, 'He raised us up together and made us sit together in the heavenly places in Christ Jesus.' Philippians 3 contains similar teaching where Paul writes in verses 9 and 10 about union in Christ's death and resurrection, and about union at the throne in verse 20 – 'Our citizenship is in heaven.'

Isaiah talks about this position in 40:31, 'Those who wait on the Lord shall renew their strength; they shall soar with wings like eagles.'

Peter implies this when in his first epistle, 2:9, he describes believers as being part of a 'royal priesthood'. John makes a similar reference in Revelation 1:6 where he talks about Jesus who 'has made us kings and priests to his God and Father'. Priesthood of course implies intercession, and kingship implies the sharing of authority at the throne.

This dimension therefore relates to spiritual warfare in which, from our 'throne' position, we can identify satanic activity and co-operate with God in His strategy for Kingdom extension, praying with authority and binding the enemy. In fact, Jesus tells us to 'bind the strong man' (Matt. 12:29). How does this work in real life? The following episodes are examples of warfare praying.

* Three missionary ladies in India notice that after they go to bed at night strange noises come from the basement. On investigation there is no apparent reason for them. They summon other nearby missionary colleagues and together they take a stand of faith against occult activity and command the demons to depart. They have no further trouble.

* In Greece an American wins a 16-year-old lad to Christ. The Greek Orthodox church takes the missionary to court where he is given a three year sentence. Christians in USA pray. An appeal is made to the supreme court. The sentence is quashed.

* Near Chicago a pastor has seen little fruit for his six years of labour in a church of seventy. He decides to fast and pray and claims a number of streets round the church for the Lord. A grotesque being appears in his room and says, 'I don't want to give you that much.' The pastor takes authority over the demon and continues to claim these streets. Three months later his church has doubled in size, most of the converts having to be delivered from demon possession.

* In 1982 Brother Andrew puts out a call for seven years of prayer for the downfall of communism. The seven years end in mid-1989. In November of that year the Berlin wall tumbles and communism is swept from Europe.

* In Pakistan two Christians are wrongfully accused of insulting Mohammed and are sentenced to death. Christians in Australia,

Britain and USA pray against the forces of evil. The Prime Minister intervenes and moves the case to a higher court where the verdict is quashed.

* The teenage daughter of a missionary couple working overseas is being cared for at home by her aunt. She is mystified by the girl's bursts of violent temper and foul language. At a convention she asks for prayer for the girl who at that moment falls to the ground writhing like a snake, and tries to bite the leg of the counsellor. After authoritative prayer a demon is cast out.

* A missionary waiting at Karachi airport is arrested for drug trafficking. Another man standing nearby whom the police found with drugs said he received them from the missionary. Earnest prayer is made for the situation in Australia and Britain. The court case proceeds for months; in the 29th week he is acquitted.

* In Colorado Springs a man asks to see the pastor of a large church. During the interview he says he hates the pastor and would be delighted to kill him. He calls the pastor names and curses his children. Then without

explanation he suddenly relaxes and says the Holy Spirit would not let him say more. At another church at that very time a group of intercessors had a heavy burden for this pastor. One of them later said he had a picture of a man with a spirit of violence and murder, so prayed quoting the scripture 'Jesus came to destroy the works of the Devil' (1 John 3:8).

* A missionary in the Philippines sees a news item on TV about a woman in prison behaving like an animal – biting, scratching, and kicking the doctors. He feels led to go to the prison and gets permission to see the woman. He casts out demons and leads her to Christ. He said afterwards that the demons said they hated him and cursed God and the blood of Christ.

* A missionary couple laboured for years in Thailand without seeing any fruit. They then decided to give one day a week to spiritual warfare against the evil spirits in the area. A wave of conversions followed.

If we have experienced the release and then the equipping of phases I and II we should now be able to meet the needs of others. We are no longer the rescued; we are the rescuers. The life, the gifting, the power and authority of God should start to flow through us by the operation of the Spirit. As Norman Grubb puts it, 'we move on from discipleship to apostleship'. Of course the enemy tries hard to convince us that this is nonsense but as we start to move into this by faith we become the soldiers of God (Greek *stratiotes*), 2 Timothy 2:3. Grubb, in *Yes, I Am* (pages 158-189), describes this third phase:

You should read the life of Rees Howells, the Welsh intercessor, to see a perfect example of how God turns a disciple into an apostle. He got Rees Howells point by point, to the place where the Holy Ghost had no rival in his life, until He had him finally fitted-out for his great life's ministry of intercession.

So we see that there must be a serious weighing-up of our position on the third level, just as there has been on the first and second. We 'count the cost', as Jesus said. We need to face the fact that it means that we don't assess life any more on the grounds of 'What do I get out of it? What happens to me?' Or 'Will I achieve what I'm meant to be?' And when things 'happen' to us in life, we no longer may say 'Why this?', as if implying we have been hardly done by. No! We see it all in terms of His fulfilling some loving and saving purpose *for others* through it, even though at the moment we cannot see that in it.

While that is the negative side of this third-level life, the positive is tremendous – so tremendous that it appears fantastic to our human sight. The positive is what Jesus taught about the Spirit's filling. It is not simply that we thirsting ones may fully drink of Him and remain filled, but Jesus says, 'Stretch your believing further. The Holy Spirit didn't come merely to fill *you*; but from *your* fullness *others* will be filled.' In other words, He is in you now as rivers of living water *flowing out from you.* 'He that believeth in me... out of his inmost centre shall flow rivers of living water' (John 7:38).

But out of us will never flow these rivers if we forget our union reality and look at ourselves in our humanity. It then becomes a joke. 'Rivers – through me?' But once again, there is only the one way – faith. I took my first step into that third level as a young man, when starting out in my call to the Congo. I was so hesitant, and it seemed so absurd that rivers of the Spirit could flow out of me, that, though I did believe, I was a bit like the man who said to Jesus, 'Lord, I believe; help thou mine unbelief.' So I said, 'Lord, I believe this word, at least for a muddy trickle to flow out!' But I did believe! And He has surely done more than I asked or thought! So *believe* – which is not one whit different from the believing in John 3:16 for salvation and in Galatians 2:20 for oneness. Stand there, laughing, maybe – as I did – at the absurdity of its ever being fulfilled. But remember: faith is substance!

We *are* now fathers, apostles, bondslaves, co-labourers, co-saviours, intercessors – and the Spirit seals it to us. It requires of us that kind of serious 'counting the cost' that Jesus spoke of in Luke 14:28. It is the taking up of our cross voluntarily (and for keeps), just as there was our coming *to* the cross and then the taking of our place *on* the cross. This is now the cross-bearing for others.

As S.D. Gordon has said, 'Prayer is the conflict; service is just picking up the spoils.' A book has been written by Rev. Stuart Robinson; its title is *Praying the Price*. This neatly identifies both the key and the cost of the 'apostleship' ministry to which Norman Grubb refers. Unless we know our way through in the strategy of the Spirit our bits of service will be as effective as pea-shooting against the Rock of Gibraltar.

CHAPTER 7

THREE KINDS OF
KINGDOM PRAYER

Section A: Strategic Praying
New Testament figure – the Soldier

The essential element of soldiering is an under-standing of and commitment to the laid-down strategy. How many church elders or deacons have learned to wait on God for His strategy for their fellowship? Most efforts along this line are simply discussions about ideas rather than waiting on God for His leading.

In a magazine article written in 1938, Grubb described the early days of WEC when staff and candidates would meet morning by morning to seek God for a revelation of His purpose. Grubb would bring a situation before them – say a survey of unreached peoples in a certain country – and then, after looking at the Scriptures and reading how men of God were guided by the Spirit, he would say, 'Now what is the Lord saying to us about this tribe?' After clarification and some discussion the fellowship would bring the matter to the Lord, seeking the witness of the Spirit regarding whatever course of action was necessary. Time after time they would rise from their knees strong in faith regarding what should be done. It wasn't a matter of asking whether we had the money or the personnel or the visas. It was simply, 'What is the Spirit seeking to convey to us?' This is how WEC grew by leaps and bounds, from a sorry, little, beleaguered group of thirty-five in one field and one sending base in 1931 to dozens of fields and hundreds of workers, within a generation. Here are a few paragraphs from that article.

It must be noted that guidance is the direct communication of the Spirit with our spirits, and is not to be confused with the Scriptures. God's written word is the general guide to His people. The Bible is the wholly inspired and infallible revelation of the principles of Christian living, and any individual guidance which does not conform to it is from a false source. Also in some cases a sentence of Scripture may be the medium by which the Spirit speaks to us. But even then the point that makes it guidance to me is its application *by the Spirit* to a given situation; its leaping, as it were, out of the book into my heart. *The Spirit* gives the guidance. It is always in conformity with the Scriptures, and may be in the words of Scripture, but it is the indwelling Spirit who guides.

We recognise and utilise the mind in its right position. The mind is a useful servant, but not the final arbiter of truth. The exaltation of human reason to the throne of authority is the sin of 'the wise of this world'.

Thus we examine thoughtfully our situation, know all that we can about it, let the Scriptures throw any light upon it, but then we refuse to make the decision. That must come from the inner witness. The best thing we can do, having stored our mind with the facts, is to leave them with God. It is not a state of forgetfulness, but a redirection of our attention. We were concentrating on the problem: now we concentrate on Him, the Solver. When our eye is single, our whole body is full of light.

For a biblical example of a strategic prayer time see Acts 13:1-3, out of which the first missionary group was created.

A mission majoring on gospel broadcasting in Asia had a very sparse mail response from one Moslem area – until recently, when a flood of letters started to come in. Then they discovered that a large church in a sending country had come to hear of the spiritual need in that region and its members had committed themselves to systematic and intensive prayer for a spiritual breakthrough.

A group of workers had a burden for evangelism in central Spain but were seeing very little fruit. They decided to give Friday afternoons to authoritative prayer for God to reveal a fruit-producing strategy.

Soon after this they noted that most of the young people who stood around their open-air meetings and who turned up at one home meeting were drug addicts. It dawned on them that the Holy Spirit was leading them into a drug rehabilitation ministry. In miraculous ways God has provided property and personnel so that there are now forty-nine such centres in the 'Betel' ministry in Spain and new thrusts are developing in Mexico, USA, Britain, Germany, France, Portugal and Italy (see *Rescue Shop Within a Yard of Hell*, and *Rescue Shop II,* published by Christian Focus Publications, Scotland).

Section B: Intercessory Praying
New Testament figure – the Priest

Just as the soldier is concerned about knowing and carrying out God's strategy, so the priest is concerned with his function as an intercessor, acting as a go-between, intimate with God but identified with man. His characteristics are:

Empathy　　　A wholehearted and imaginative entering into the feelings of the one being prayed for. Paul was so burdened for his fellow Jews he said he was willing to be cursed if it would mean that his brothers would have their eyes opened to their need of Christ. Rom. 9:3.

Continuity

The capacity to 'hang in there' until the need has been met. (See Moses on the mountain during the battle with the Amalekites. Exod. 17.)

Intensity

Willingness to be moved by the Spirit into intense prayer. Such was Epaphras who is described in Col. 4:12 as 'wrestling' (Greek – agonising) in prayer for the Colossian believers. The same root – *agonia* – is used about Jesus when he sweated drops of blood in Gethsemane. Luke 22:44.

Responsibility

The intercessor differs from the pray-er because he accepts the responsibility for another. He cannot give up until God removes his commission. After discovering that the Israelites had made a golden calf in his absence, Moses goes into the presence of God and says in effect, 'Lord blot me out, only give them another chance' (Exod. 32:32).

For a biblical example of an intercessory prayer time see Acts 12:5-16.

Section C: Confrontational Prayer
New Testament figure – the King

The supreme characteristic of kingship is authority, and the New Testament has abundant teaching on the fact that the believer is given a position of authority against the powers of darkness. It is an authority based on Satan's defeat at the Cross and in the resurrection. 'They overcame him by the blood of the Lamb' (Rev. 12:11). 'For this purpose the Son of God was manifest that he might loose us from the works of the devil' (1 John 3:8). '...that through death he might destroy him that had the power of death, that is, the devil' (Heb. 2:14).

Seven times in John 14, 15, 16 Jesus encourages His disciples to pray in His name, that is, pray with His delegated authority.

A number of Christians in Britain who had colleagues working in Burkino Faso, West Africa, were horrified to learn from them that once the young men of a certain tribe went through the heathen initiation ceremonies they became virtually impervious to the gospel, so powerful were the evil forces they encountered in the process. A group decided to give time to authoritative intercession against these satanic powers. By the time the next set of ceremonies came along two of the chiefs involved had been converted, two others had died and the government had stepped in and reduced the length of the rites from a month to just a few days. Not yet total victory, but a vast improvement on what had prevailed up to that time.

Rev. Noel and Mrs Phyl Gibson of Sydney have had a tremendous ministry in helping Christians who have been subject to satanic attack and invasion. They have given permission to relate these incidents from their book, *Evicting Demonic Squatters and Breaking Bondages*, pages 60, 85 and 106 of the 1987 edition:

A married woman regarded herself as a 95% ideal marriage partner but the 5% failure area became so troublesome that she felt it was putting her marriage in jeopardy. When troublesome hereditary spirits were cast out a sweet change took place in her, bringing her to a new security in which her contribution to the marriage was greatly enhanced.

A young man who claimed to be a Christian became very arrogant during counselling, claiming he had never sinned. His father, paternal grandfather, maternal grandfather and great-grandfather had all been staunch Freemasons. The Masonic spirits were cast out and the young man was sent away to seek God about his true spiritual condition. Twelve hours later he returned, broken and repentant. In a flood of tears he was born again and showed an immediate change of lifestyle.

For several years it has been the writers' privilege to minister to ethnic Chinese students from various countries (in E. Asia). They are nearly always first generation Christians, and their cultural bondages and dominations include spirits of Buddhism, Taoism, Confucianism and spirits of ancestor worship. After (deliverance) ministry the release of emotion and warmth they exhibit is quite remarkable.

The key issue in each of these incidents was the *authority* exercised by the counsellors over satanic powers.

For a biblical example of a warfare prayer meeting see Acts 4:18-31. For an instance of demon ejection see Acts 16:16-18.

Too often our prayers are at the asking-hoping level when they should be at the perceiving-believing-receiving level. Here are some contrasts between what we might call 'normal' praying versus 'throne' praying:

NORMAL PRAYING	THRONE PRAYING
1. Asks	1. Receives (Mark 11:24)
2. Hopes	2. Believes (Mark 11:24)
3. Pleads	3. Praises (Romans 4:20)
4. Is uncertain	4. Knows (Colossians 1:9)
5. Uses rationality	5. Has authority (John 14–16)
6. Based on desire	6. Bases on revelation (Hebrews 11:13)
7. Majors on problems/difficulties	7. Understands spiritual warfare (Matthew 12:29)
8. Addresses the throne	8. Declares *from* the throne (Colossians 3:2)
9. Is confined to the immediate	9. Relates to the strategic
10. Seeks to persuade God	10. Co-operates with God (Acts 4:29-31)

Normal praying is not wrong; much of our routine praying is of this nature but we must be alert, as occasion demands, to move by faith into authoritative and expectant prayer, especially when faced with opposition, resistance to the Gospel and other forms of satanic activity.

What exactly are the resources available to the Christian who is prepared to enter spiritual conflict for the extension of the Lord's Kingdom? Here is a brief summary!

1. The blood of Christ (Heb. 2:14-15, Rev.12:11)
2. The name of Jesus (Acts 3:16, 16:18)
3. Overcoming faith (1 John 5:4)
4. The Sword of the Spirit (Eph. 6:17, Heb. 4:12)
5. All other parts of the armour (Eph. 6:12-17)
6. All kinds of prayer (Eph. 6:18)
7. Unity of believers (Acts 4:32).

ELEMENTS OF KINGDOM PRAYING

TYPE OF PRAYER	KEY IDEAS	LEVEL OF FAITH	BIBLICAL FIGURE	OBJECTIVE	BIBLICAL EXAMPLE
STRATEGIC	Waiting on God Awareness of His will Co-operation with God	Creative faith	Soldier	Kingdom's Extension	Antioch Church Acts 13 Paul Acts 16:9
INTER-CESSORY	Respons-ibility Continuity Intensity Empathy	Claiming faith	Priest	God's intervention	Jerusalem Church Acts 12 Epaphras Col. 4:12
CON-FRONTAT-IONAL	Recognition of enemy Resistance Reliance on resources (see previous page) Rejection of Satanic forces	Conquering faith	King	Satan's expulsion	Jerusalem Church, Acts 4 Paul, Acts 16:18

54

CHAPTER 8

ENTERING IN

Do these truths live in our experience? Our lifestyle? Jesus said in John 8:32 that truth liberates, but it can only do so when we 'marry' it, when we embrace the reality of the concepts and apply them in life situations.

For many the moment of revelation becomes the moment of confrontation. Will we walk away from this as too costly, too jarring, too radical? Or will we take the plunge?

Here are three stories to illustrate how others have allowed the truth of union with Christ to affect their lifestyle in a radical way. Names are changed to preserve anonymity.

Hilda was a missionary in Central Asia – one of a team of five – whose goal was to gain access to a forbidden land and provide medical services as a means of reaching the people. Here is her personal story:

'The only real problem for me was that I could not get along with Marion, one of my co-workers. Everything she did annoyed me! Yet I had to recognise that she was the one that God used to bring people through to a new or a more vital relationship with Himself, whether they were raw heathen, nominal Christians, or missionaries.

'But for me, things would go along peacefully for just so long. Then I would explode, trying to change Marion or put her straight. Of course, afterwards there were tears, repentance, and pleas for forgiveness. I knew the value of the Bible teaching on 'walking in the light' (1 John 1:7), but the same problem would keep building up in me. I hated myself. I couldn't blame the others. My reactions were the problem. I even thought of leaving the field, but I knew I would only take myself with me wherever I went.

'At home there had been inspiring Christian meetings, which had been like spiritual props. Back there I had gathered the impression I was somewhat spiritual. But here, stripped of all that, there didn't seem to be much spirituality left. The climax came one day when the field leader called me in for a chat. "Hilda," he began, "we want to send a team to the border. This will be our next advance. We feel it best that Elizabeth and Marion go, and that you stay here with my wife who, as you know, is pregnant. I have to go away for a month or two on business, but will be back as soon as I can. It wouldn't be advisable for you, or good for the work, if you went into the new territory, because of this relationship problem."

'I went to my room alone. "So this is it!" I

meditated. "I, who was going to do such big things with God, am held back not by mountains, rigorous climate, bandits, nor even lack of government permits, but by *myself*! I'm a liability to God, not an asset!"

'Then in keeping with His sense of humour, God used Marion to help me. She came to me one day. We went out to talk in the back yard, all bundled up in winter clothing. As soon as she began, I knew every word was from God. "You have been examining yourself, looking for some root of evil that causes your reactions. But you dealt with those in your previous experiences with God. Your problem now is your 'good self'."

'"What!" I exclaimed, "How can 'good' be 'bad'?"

'"Well," she said, "you have natural, strong qualities, and you have been working from your natural humanity – that nature which was tainted at the Fall. You've been functioning from what the Bible calls 'the flesh', meaning that old nature. God can't use that for His purposes. Only what is born of God's Spirit is of any use to God. He has been showing you this, and the difference between the two."

'I saw she was right. God illuminated it to my spirit. She went on, "Jesus died on the cross for this nature also, for Romans 6 tells us that we were included with all our enemies, inner and outer, in the death of Jesus. He dealt with them all to set us free. He didn't deal just with our sins but with our basic fallen nature, and all our other enemies. You must die to all of your old self and its ways and preferences. Let the Lord put it all to death as you give it to Him. No one can crucify himself. But you and I *were* crucified with Him – potentially – 2000 years ago. Believe it, give up, surrender, and receive all He did for us. All that is useful to God is His Son, ministered in us and through us, by the Holy Spirit. Die to all else."

'So I wrote out all the facts about the "good self" as well as those of the "bad self" and then across the lot I scribbled the words of Galatians 2:20, "I am crucified with Christ." It was a cold-blooded transaction with God, with no emotion beyond the original desolation and repentance. But I knew it was God's time. He meant business with me, and I certainly meant business with Him. We agreed together about it! I knew I had to believe that God would do His part. My part was to cease from struggling, and believe what He had already done, identifying with it.

'How did it work out?

'The next morning at the breakfast table someone presented me with a drawing of a tombstone, mounted over a nice grassy mound. On the stone was written, "Hilda died...", and the previous day's date. I kept that to present to the devil in case he forgot I really had died!

'It wasn't long before he tried to make me

forget. Marion did something I didn't like, and the old feelings began to come to the surface. Not trusting myself to stay with Marion, I fled to my room and, on my knees, began to mumble Colossians 3:3, "I am dead and my life is hid with Christ in God." I meant business, and so did God. "I don't have to behave like this any more. That old nature is not me!" I cried. Suddenly, as though a balloon had been pricked, all the horrible feelings evaporated. I knew I loved Marion again – which, after all, was what I really felt for her. I hadn't wished her ill, only that she would improve! What a relief! Something had really worked. In fact, it worked every time. But if I tried other methods, they didn't work at all.

'Not long after, a new awareness began to dawn, so sweet and glorious, "It's really 'Christ in me the hope of glory!' Yes, it really is! He in me can do it all, He really can. Anything necessary to fulfil His will, He can do even in *me*. I just need to get out of the way so He can function." '

Another who has carried heavy responsibilities in mission administration writes:

'Following two years' service in the air force, I returned to banking, was converted and called to WEC and mission. I went to the Missionary Training College in Glasgow. With no evangelical background, I really needed Bible training. I was at times confused by the different theological

59

schools of thought but MTC helped me greatly, and I began to understand what it meant to die with Christ, to die to my old nature, to know the fullness of the Spirit, and to live a sanctified life. But... I was only paddling in the shallows. Norman Grubb, on a couple of visits, really stirred me to see how much more there was, but after he departed, I was left with a great appreciation for his teaching but with little experience of it!

'Through Romans 12:1-2, I moved a step closer, but to my shame, during the next twenty years I was still having up and down experiences even though I was called to leadership positions. Those who looked on the outside never saw the internal struggles, the self-effort, the trying to be what people expected me to be.

'As a Regional Adviser for a large area, I blamed God for always stretching me too much, and for making me do things for which I was not equipped or gifted. Occasions such as difficult interviews just screwed me up inside. It came to a head in one country when a big convention was coming up. I looked forward to seeing this event, and to taking some good photos, until I learned that I was to be the speaker/evangelist! It was just the situation I dreaded. My daily reading, in the RSV at the time, two days before the event, was 2 Corinthians 5:20: "So we are ambassadors for Christ, God making his appeal through us." It was the "appeal" bit that caught me. That was what I feared – that no one would respond to my appeal, and my inadequacy would be revealed yet again! During the previous months I had been reading *Who Am I?* by Norman Grubb. I was into my third reading, trying to move truths down from my head to my heart. I had written in the flyleaf of my Bible this quotation: "My need therefore is not to have more, but to possess my possessions, to know who I am, not who I ought to become, not to acquire, but to recognise."

'Now I was cornered! I needed to be! I went down on my knees, gave up my struggles, and recognised the fact that He *did* live in me – and I in Him; that I was inadequate but He in me was more than adequate; that I did not have love, but that He could love through me.

'When I stood up to preach, I knew it did not matter whether anyone from the 3000 strong crowd responded or not. God would make *His* "appeal" through me.

'Within days of returning to base, my wife said publicly that she had a new husband! If she was relieved to be living with a different man – so was I! These past nearly twenty years have been a totally different story in every way. I just regret that I wasted so much time. Sharing "union" has become the main plank of my ministry. I used to be a frantic "do-er". Now I am a "be-er" first. "Doing" has to follow from that. Now I know who I am – not who I (or others) think I ought to be!'

Another Christian worker who has had a powerful ministry in S.E. Asia for many years shares his testimony:

'When I finished Bible College my one desire was to go to the Wycliffe linguistic course and then straight out to the mission field. But my dad wrote and said, "I think God is going to call you back to the farm for a time." That was the last thing I wanted, but on that very day the Lord spoke to me through Habakkuk 2:3, "The vision is for an appointed time;... though it tarry, wait for it."

'I went back and worked on my own on a farm that my dad had bought. (He was now living in the city). Every night once I had finished my evening meal I would read and read the Scriptures till one in the morning, because I was searching for reality.

'I knew I was forgiven; I knew the power of the blood to cleanse, but my life was a round of sin, confession, struggle and falling again. That was when the Lord started to show me the marvellous truth of Union with Christ.

'I read *The Normal Christian Life* by Watchman Nee, *In Christ* by A.J. Gordon, and *Born Crucified* by L.E. Maxwell, but there was something I just could not grasp. I really was in Romans 7. Then I came across Paul's prayer in Ephesians 1 and decided to pray it every day. "Lord, give me the spirit of wisdom and revelation in the knowledge of Christ, the eyes of my understanding being enlightened..."

'One morning I was reading about the death of Christ and His body being put in the tomb. The Lord gently whispered to my spirit. (It was a very quiet moment; I had a sense of awe – as if time stood still.) "Did Christ really die?" "Oh yes, Lord, He really did." "So did you, because you were in Him when He died." Suddenly my eyes were opened. I saw it. I did not have to struggle to get into Him. I was already in Him. I had to learn to abide. I had died with Christ. I was buried with Christ. I was raised with Christ. I was seated with Christ in the heavenlies – and this opened the whole area of spiritual warfare.

'Christ had not only dealt with my sin, He had dealt with me as the sinner. He had defeated Satan. Now I was seated with Him, in the place of authority over the powers of darkness.

'These things became key truths in my ministry in S.E. Asia, for the next thirty years.'

Rowland Croucher, a well-known Australian pastor who specialises in an encouragement ministry to fellow pastors, contacted a number of groups and asked them, "What's the Big Idea in Paul's preaching/writings?"

Here are the responses:
Lutherans: Justification by faith.
Reformed Churches: The electing grace of God.

Pentecostals: The power of the indwelling Spirit.
Fundamentalists: Salvation from sin.
Wesleyan/Holiness groups: The sanctifying work of the Spirit.

Croucher concludes: 'All the above doctrines are means to the end of being "united with Christ" – the great goal of the Christian, and of the universe. When they become ends in themselves they fall short of God's holy intention for His people.'

Let's go for God's full intention!